WRITING FOR THE KINDLE

A 3-BOOK SERIES ON SELF-PUBLISHING AND PROMOTING EBOOKS ON AMAZON

BY RON KNESS

ISBN: 1481860100

ISBN-13: 978-1481860109

Table of Contents

How to Self-Publish Your Ebook on Amazon

The Nuts and Bolts, Step-by-Step Guide to Self-Publishing Freedom

Getting published has been a childhood dream many of us have had for a long time. In the past without an agent or a "book deal", for most of us that is what it was - a dream. Then came along the Kindle e-reader from Amazon and all of that changed. Today, anyone can achieve "Published Author" status whether you are a writer or not. More on the "or not" part later.

As a writer, you are either a fan of Amazon or you are not. Now don't get me wrong, Amazon is not perfect and they do have some strict criteria (which in the end is good for all of us), but you are not going to beat them, so why not join them and get your ebook(s) listed (for free) in the biggest online marketplace in the world.

Why Target E-books for Kindle?

This is a question I get asked a lot. To carry it one-step further, *"Why write an e-book for Kindle and not just for any e-book reader?"*

As part of my answer, let me use the facts and figures that appeared in a 2010 article based on an interview with Jeff Bezos, CEO and founder of Amazon:

• Once Amazon reduced its Kindle price from $259 to $189, the sale of Kindle e-readers tripled.

• Total sales of Kindle e-books tripled as well from the first 6 months of 2009 to the first 6 months of 2010; it is safe to **assume all those new Kindle owners are also actively buying e-books**.

• Kindle ebook sales have outpaced hardcover books. Amazon sells 183 Kindle-ebooks for every 100 hardcover books sold.

• Amazon began selling hardcover books over 15 years ago while they only started selling Kindle e-books forty-plus months ago. It is interesting to note that Amazon's hardcover sales are still steadily increasing; it just so happens that Kindle sales are outpacing hardcover sales at a much faster rate. However, if you want to expand your writing career to include print publishing on Amazon via CreateSpace, that is another outlet for your work and another stream of money to pursue, but not the focus of this ebook. It is however, included in my report Beyond Kindle.

So let's move on to how to publish your ebook on Amazon. Self-publishing in this venue is an eight-step process and it starts way before you even write your first word.

The steps are:

1. Picking a topic

2. Researching topic viability

3. Writing

4. Formatting

5. Creating an ebook cover

6. Creating an Amazon KDP Account

7. Pricing

8. Promoting

Step 1 - Picking a Topic

Writing an ebook that will sell on Amazon starts by researching to see what types of ebooks are currently selling well. For an ebook to perform, there has to be a lot of interest in the form of Amazon and Internet searches on that topic. Research does not have to be a time-consuming process, however, the time you do put into it will pay you back many times over in additional sales.

How to Find Out What Sells

Below are several resources you can use to research current hot topics. These are the best digital content marketplaces the Internet has to offer. You only have to know the keywords used in your chosen niche to find out which ebook topics are selling like hotcakes.

Jungle-Search.com

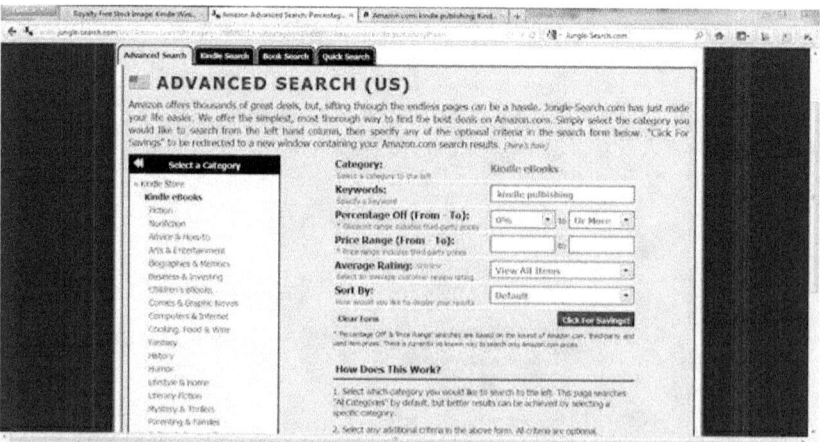

You can get a lot of in-depth information from this site. What's more, it offers listings for other languages as well, which would be a good thing if you are targeting a bilingual market or you plan on producing your ebook in multiple language formats. You can also search by category or subject (sub-niche), price range, reader age and many other factors.

To use Jungle-Search, just select a category from the left side of the screen, enter relevant keywords and click on Click for Savings button.

Clickbank.com

Many e-book writers prefer to sell their digital content (and hardcopy books for that matter) via Clickbank's Marketplace. Just click on *Marketplace* at the top of the screen and enter your keyword(s).

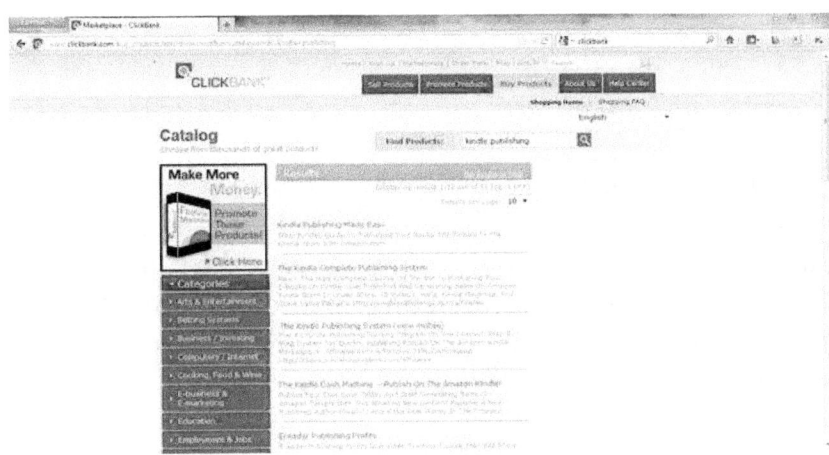

ReaderIQ.com

It has many similar features to Jungle -Search and it also
allows you to search according to review ratings. In any
case, if there is something you cannot find at Jungle-
Search, this website is a good alternative to check out.

NovelRank.com

This is a very simple website compared to the other sites
mentioned, but sometimes simple really works best. In
this case, Novel Rank will help you track the sales of any
book or ebook sold on Amazon – including yours. What's
more, it can also track your sales in Amazon sites for
other countries like France and Germany.

Amazon.com

Last but not least, do not forget to check out Amazon's own ranking for e-books in your niche. They also offer the best reviews since most Kindle readers are less inclined to visit other websites to post a review when they can do so right in Amazon.

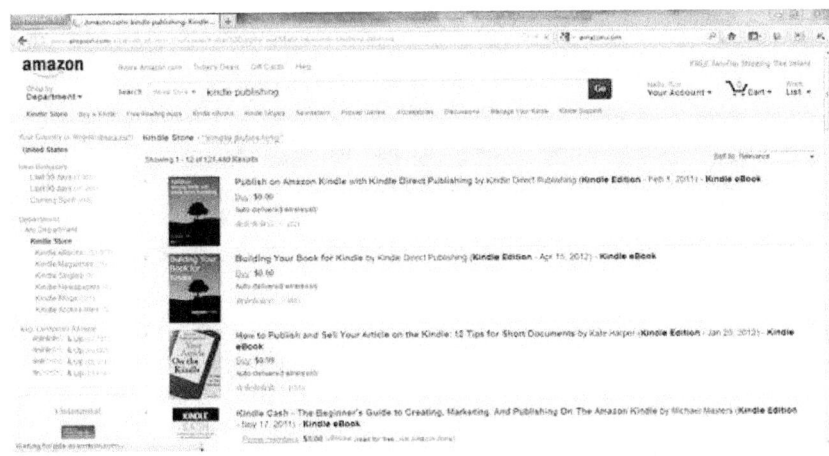

Keep in mind that each website has its own pros and cons, and the information contained in each of the search results will vary depending on what type of information you are looking for. The best advice is to use of all of these websites when searching for your ebook's topic. Besides, they are all free!

If you do not find a lot of sales in your chosen topic, then you most likely would be better off choosing a more popular topic. Don't be apprehensive if you find a lot of competition in your topic - competition is good! We'll address in the next chapter how to make your ebook stand out in the crowd.

Step 2 - Research Topic Viability

In the last chapter, you were able to find out both what kind of competition you are going up against with your future ebook and how tough it is. At this point, you have either become more confident or worried about your ebook and ultimately, prospective sales.

If you are already confident about your e-book topic and its chances of selling well, then great, because what you are about to learn will make your confidence level go even higher. If you are worried, don't be – we'll show you a way to make your ebook rise up in the rankings.

First and foremost, your ebook needs to be different than the rest of them on the same topic. If you are a green ball in a sea of green balls, you all look the same. But if you are a red ball in that same sea, you stick out like a sore thumb. To sell digital content, you have to be found. To be found, you have to get noticed – you have to be that red ball.

To get noticed, you have to do something that all the other ebooks on your topic were not able to accomplish. At first glance, this may sound impossible when you are writing about, say, something as broad as Internet marketing. But read on.

Based on the number of ebooks in your target market, it probably seems like anybody with even a hint of experience on that topic thinks s/he has mind-altering advice to offer to readers. They do not, but you do! You just have to ask yourself the following questions and then choose which ones you believe you can answer more satisfactorily with your ebook:

•   What topics were left out in the other e-books that you can cover?

•   If many of the ebooks are talking about the same things in your chosen topic, then how about choosing something slightly different.

•   If your topic is about blog marketing, how about covering the topic of vlogging (video blogging) or using Pinterest for marketing instead, for example.

•   If you want to cover the same topic, what can you do to make your e-book do a better job at explaining the subject matter?

•   When you write about your topic, be sure to explain both the features **and** benefits buyers will get from reading your ebook. From the buyer's perspective, answer their question "What's in it for me?"

Unique Content

Other e-books most likely have covered the exact same topic, but you can prove to your perspective buyers that yours is better – or even the best version. Start with a killer title (more about how to do this later). Then don't forget to include an excerpt from your ebook via your marketing efforts as well as a short bullet list of what they can expect to learn in the form of a blurb of your ebook. Blurbs are typically like the back cover teaser found on most hardcover books.

What kind of perspective can you use that the other ebooks on that topic have not yet covered? You can also present your content as unique and different by choosing a not-yet-covered angle or slant. There are a couple of ways to do this; you have to determine for yourself which one would work better for you and your target market.

Method #1: You can make generalized content more specific or oriented towards a sub or micro-niche. For example, instead of writing about the broad topic of social media, you can write about how the reader can use Twitter, or Facebook, or Pinterest in marketing their business. Or write an ebook on each of them and make it a series. Then do as I have done with this book and combine the three into a Print On Demand (POD) trilogy.

Method #2: Make same content appeal to a more specific group of people. For example, Twitter, Facebook and Pinterest are primarily used by non-business people. Write an ebook on how to take primarily personal social media venues and make them work as marketing tools for business.

For now, stay writing with what you know; your ebook will be much better if you write on topics that you have direct experience with. That way you can include real-life examples and tried-and-true tips. When writing on these topics, your passion for the topic will come through in your writing!

Unique Titles

If you have tried researching about writing titles before, then you may have noticed that advice from different "experts" can be quite contradictory.

Personally, I follow a basic ebook title formula, which can be divided into two steps:

- Step 1: Follow the KISS rule (keep it short and simple) and include your primary keyword in your title.

- Step 2: Elaborate by using secondary keywords, numbers, and trigger words in your tagline or secondary title. You will notice that most non-fiction books use this method. Why? Because it works!

Titles function like headlines and attention-grabbers, but they cannot paint the whole picture alone, without a sub-headline or secondary title. You will notice both these rules have been adhered to even with this very guide you are reading.

Primary Title:

How to Self-Publish Your Ebook on Amazon

Secondary Title:

The Nuts and Bolts, Step-by-Step Guide to Self-Publishing Freedom

We were going for the keyword of self-publish. It appears in both the title and sub-title. Once we create a new ebook on Amazon, you will see where this is important.

As for other guidelines when writing unique titles that will sell an ebook, use the list of tips below. It is possible that all or just some of them may apply to the ebook you want to write.

•	Make a list of short-tail keywords/keyword phrases that you can use for your title. Short-tail keywords are the ones having the highest search results.

•	Look to the titles from bestselling ebooks in your chosen niche for inspiration and ideas.

•	Consider using the lingo of your target market when composing your title. They may search using some of these words.

•	Make your ebook stand out in the pack by creating a title that people will never forget. That is the first part of making your ebook unique and different from the others.

Use thought-provoking "trigger" phrases in your titles such as:

•	The Secret to _____

•	How to _____

•	How to _____ in [insert number] Easy Steps

•	Top [insert number] Ways to _____

•	Top [insert number] Reasons to _____

•	Everything You Ever Wanted to Know About _____

Step 3 - Writing an Ebook That Sells

When preparing to write your ebook, you have to decide if you want to entertain your readers or inform them. Deciding between one or the other will give you a clearer goal of your ebook.

Knowing which one you want your ebook to do will help you determine which bits and pieces of your research are the most valuable. Some ebooks try to straddle both lines; keep in mind that you will have a more challenging road ahead of you if you attempt to satisfy both types of readers in the same ebook.

Also, contrary to what some people may think, fluff pieces (especially romance and historical fiction) do sell. These are perfect examples of ebooks that entertain instead of inform. Readers of these ebooks want to be entertained and usually have no hopes of learning anything from their reading, so fluff satisfies that need – end of story. However, most ebooks that inform don't contain fluff as those readers expect facts, figures and information that they can use to solve a problem or to learn how to do something.

Write Your Own E-book

You can use the tips below to help write your ebook. From your research (or personal experience on the topic), you already have all the material, and probably more than you can use, to write a great ebook. Next, you have to organize the material in a logical sequence so that it has a beginning (tell them what you are going to tell them), middle (tell them), and an end (tell them what you told them) – so that your writing "flows".

1. Start with an outline

The easiest way to organize your ebook is to create an outline. You may add to it, or delete from it, or modify it as you go along, so don't think you have to get it perfect the first time out. Change it on the fly as you develop your thoughts. This isn't as traumatic as outlining was in your English classes and nobody is going to grade it, so have fun with it. By the time you finish your outline, you should have a good idea as to how you will structure your ebook.

2. Take your time when writing the Introduction.

This is the make-or-break, life-or-death part of your ebook, so give it the attention it deserves. Amazon, along with most e-book-selling websites, allows readers to view the first pages of your work, and that usually includes your introduction. Just select an ebook on Amazon.com and click on *Look Inside* button and you will see what I mean.

Readers will take advantage of such opportunities – I know I do when I'm looking at buying an ebook or hard cover.

<u>If you lose them in your Introduction, you lost them for good, along with a sale.</u>

So to that end, keep the following tips in mind when writing an introduction:

•   Use facts, figures and other information your readers can use after they read your ebook. (You will note that I used this strategy in my own Introduction in this ebook as well.)

•   Lay the groundwork for your ebook, whether it is to entertain or inform. In other words *"tell them what you are going to tell them"* in your introduction.

•   Give them just a taste of what to expect – whet their appetite, if you will - and your readers will end up buying your ebook to get the "rest of the story".

3. Worry about the middle.

If the information in any of your middle chapters can be condensed or eliminated completely, do it! Just *"tell them what you want to tell them"*, so you keep their attention the whole way through. Otherwise your readers may feel cheated and not buy from you again.

4. Bring it to an end.

Did you accomplish what you set out to do with your ebook? The conclusion is a good place to review (*"tell them what you told them"*) and wrap up what you have left to say about the topic. It is also a great place to include a **call-to-action** – something you want them to do next. It can be implement the steps you just laid out or information on how to buy your next ebook.

In reviewing your work, if you feel you have not addressed all of your readers anticipated goals, then revise until you get things right.

5. Revise and keep revising!

Don't rely on just your own judgment on the topic. Give out review copies to friends and colleagues before you publish it and ask for their honest opinion. Then revise based on their feedback.

After all, they are readers just like the ones who will buy your ebook. If you satisfy their expectations, your readers should be satisfied also.

Hire a Ghostwriter

If you feel that writing an ebook on your own is too daunting, too time-consuming or you are not a writer, consider hiring a ghostwriter instead.

You can search for a ghostwriter on the following websites:

- **Craigslist.com**

- **Elance.com**

- **Business Writing Resources.com**

You can get a list of other websites by Googling "ghostwriter". If you write a job listing for a ghostwriter, make sure it contains the following information:

- Writing and non-writing skills, and specialized knowledge you require from the writer.

- Level of experience in writing ebooks in general and for ebooks in your niche topic.

- Deadline for the project.

- Price or compensation range for the project.

- Ask for a resume and samples of previous work.

To further narrow your list of applicants, you may want to try the following:

- Interview candidates online and see which ones you feel you will enjoy working with – and vice versa.

- Ask for a one-page or 300-word sample for one of the sub-topics covered in your e-book to get a feel for their "voice" and writing style. You want your ghostwriter to be very similar to the style and voice that normally comes through your writing. That way, at least you won't have to edit that part.

Using Public Domain Products

When writing an ebook that you will market on Amazon, be extremely careful about using public domain materials as Amazon started cracking down on authors who use this material. The price you pay for getting caught can vary from getting your ebook taken off Amazon all the way up to you as a writer being banned *forever* from listing on Amazon again. Don't do it – it is not worth the risk.

What you can do is use public domain material as part of your research material and then use the facts, figures and relevant data in your ebook; give it a modern twist or a slant from a different angle than what has been written before by other authors on the topic. You will see this done successfully by many good fiction writers, especially with historical fiction.

Step 4 - Formatting Your Ebook

Formatting isn't the words you use or how you use them, but instead it deals with the setting of margins, type of font, size and color, as well as bulleted lists, highlighting and much more.

However, formatting can be one of the most underappreciated, and therefore overlooked, elements of ebook writing. This is unfortunate, because proper formatting can take just a bunch of words on a page and make them come alive. Also, it is one of the easiest parts of ebook writing to master. Overlooking this part of creating an ebook for Kindle and you will have massive problems trying to get your ebook to convert properly down the road. Give it the attention it deserves!

With formatting there is little need for you to use your creative side, if you don't want to. Most formatting follows set technical guidelines that once you learn, you only have to follow. However, there is wiggle-room should you choose to show some formatting creativeness. If this is your first ebook for Kindle, keep it simple and avoid getting creative.

Formatting an ebook for Kindle is pretty straightforward and only has a few rules. Therefore, this part of the chapter is one of the simpler ones in this guide. Here are the most important rules that you should consider applying when formatting your ebook:

• New Kindles render text, graphics or photos in full color. If your ebook is read on an older Kindle, colors will show up as gray, black and white anyway.

• Minimize use of graphics and photos as much as you can. If you choose to include these and once you have your ebook file complete, make sure to preview them carefully using the **Kindle Previewer** software to see how they would look after conversion. In some cases, Previewer may not show everything exactly as it ends up being after you upload your ebook file and it converts, but it will be close.

• Accepted file formats for in-book graphics and photos (not covers) are JPEG, BMP, PNG and GIF with a maximum file size of 127KB. The reason there is a difference between in-book and cover images in that they are uploaded separately, so don't include your cover as part of your ebook file.

Starting your file

Below are some simple layout tips that will make creating your ebook easier. You may not see the value of these right now, but you will once you try and convert your ebook to the Kindle format:

• **Indenting** - When setting up your paragraphs, decide on whether you want indented first lines or block style (first character of each paragraph aligned with the left margin). Don't use both. Indents are normally used for fiction and much non-fiction, whereas the block style is used only for non-fiction.

    o Don't use the tab key or space bar to create first line paragraph indents. Instead, define an indent in your paragraph style.

o   If you choose to use block style, **do not** add paragraph returns to create a blank line between paragraphs. If you are using Microsoft Word, click on the *Page Layout* from the top-line menu. Then click on the arrow in the lower right corner of the *Paragraph* option block. Next set your *Spacing After* option to the number of spaces you want between paragraphs. Usually a 6 or 12pt. trailing space after the end of each paragraph looks nice.

• **Paragraph Returns** – Keep the "hard returns" (done by hitting the Enter key) to no more than 4. Otherwise, blank pages may be created when reading your ebook on small-screened devices.

• **Paragraph Separation** –Keep your paragraphs and sentences short. Most readers dislike long paragraphs and if they submit a negative review based on that fact, it can severely hurt your sales. To create a separation between chapters, use the *Page Break* option from the *Insert tab* on the top-line menu.

• **Font Selection** – Use only simple single standard fonts in black, such as Times New Roman, Garamond or Arial in a 12 to 14 pt. You can use up to a 28 pt. for chapter titles. Do not use anything fancy, such as symbols, emoticons, etc., as they most likely will not convert correctly. If you need to highlight certain texts, do so sparingly by either underlining, using italics or bolding.

• Style – In general, do not use:

o   columns.

o   tables.

o   text boxes. NOTE: If you do have to use columns, tables or text boxes, first convert them to images and then insert them.

o   multiple fonts or paragraph styles for your body. Use Normal style for text, Headings 1 and 2 for chapter headings and subheading respectively. Using these heading settings will make creating a Table of Contents (TOC) easier too.

o   headers or footers

Do not use a Table of Contents if your e-book is just a few chapters long. If you choose to use a TOC, make sure that you use the Headings tag so that they can also serve as navigational links.

A Table of Contents looks differently in an ebook slated to be a Kindle. A Kindle TOC looks like this:

Introduction

Step 1 - Picking a Topic

Step 2 - Research Topic Viability

Step 3 - Writing an Ebook That Sells

Step 4 - Formatting Your Ebook

Step 5 - Creating Your Ebook Cover

Step 6 - Creating Your Amazon KDP Account

Step 7 - Pricing Your Ebook

Step 8 - Promoting Your Ebook

Conclusion

- Of course the difference is the Kindle TOC does not use page numbers. Remember why? (Reflowing of text when changing e-reader font size.)

- Make good use of sub-headings, bulleted or numbered lists – or any other way to further break down your data into easily read and understood points as I have done throughout this guide. Don't you agree it makes it easier to read?

- Do not forget to convert essential parts and text to internal links especially in the following places:

    * Title page

    * All calls to action; especially the one in the last chapter of your ebook that takes them to the squeeze or sales page of your next ebook.

    * Contact details

    * Invitation to subscribe or join

To align images with text, right click on the image and then click on *Format Picture – Advanced - In Line* with Text. Then center the image using Word's center button.

Once you have your file in final form, turn on the paragraph marker. It looks like a backward P in the top right corner of the *Paragraph* section.

Take out any non-essential paragraph markers. Finally, click on the *Save As* button. Select the file type as "Web Page, Filtered. This will create an HTML file which is the file format needed to convert your ebook to the Kindle format.

If you did use images in your ebook, then when you saved your ebook as an HTML, a folder containing images was also created. Put your HTML file and image folder together in a zipped folder.

To do this, first right click on your HTML file. Scroll over to the *Send To* option on the menu and click on *Compressed (zipped) Folder*. A new folder with your file name will appear with the zipped symbol on it. Now drag your image folder into the zipped folder. You will need the zipped folder (with both your HTML and images) when you go to upload your ebook and convert it.

Step 5 - Creating Your Ebook Cover

Just like "clothes make the man", so does a cover make the ebook. You have also heard that "the first impression is a lasting one"? Well, your ebook cover is your readers' first impression of your ebook, so you want to make it "pop". The best way to see what works and what does not is to visit Amazon's Kindle ebook site and look at different ebook covers and the ebook rankings. When you find one that is ranking high and that stops you dead in your tracks, examine why it caught your attention when dozens of others did not.

You want to replicate that cover design for your ebook – I didn't say copy it, but replicate it. Look at the colors used both for the background (or image or both) and text. Most likely they will contrast with each other. With ebook covers, you want to make sure that your front cover *looks completely professional*.

If you are not comfortable creating your own cover, you can hire it done by a graphic designer. You can find someone on a variety of sites, such as Fiverr.com or ; just Google "ebook cover design". You could also list your design job on one of many work sites, such as Elance.com.

For a dynamic attention-getting cover, here are some unique creation tips to keep in mind:

-       Less is more – Don't try to put too many elements on your cover. Start with a good representative digital image that takes up the whole page and then place your text accordingly on the image.

-       Or you can use a solid background, center your image on top of the background and use text boxes above and below your image. Remember, regardless of how you end up doing it, all you need is a cover image, the title (and sub-title if you have one) and the author – that's it. You can put it together using something as simple (and free) as Microsoft's Paint program or the more dynamic Microsoft Publisher. Just be sure to save your cover as a JPEG or TIFF.

-       Accepted file formats for ebook covers are TIFF and JPEG. Your cover must be *at least 1,000 pixels* on the longest side and ideally a height/width ratio of 1.6 - for example 625 pixels by 1,000 pixels. You can use images as large as 2,500 pixels on the longest side.

-       If you don't already have an image that works, buy one off of any of the royalty-free image sites, such as **Dreamstime.com**, **iStockPhoto.com**, or **Shutterstock.com**. Don't use just any image you find on the Internet, as you could be (and most likely) violating copyright laws. Do it right and buy the royalty-free rights to use the image.

-       When choosing a cover image, be sure that it is symbolic of your ebook topic. The prospective buyer should "get it" at first glance.

In the standalone version of this ebook, I chose a gray design for the background, a purchased image in the middle and text boxes above and below the image. In other ebooks, I have used this design as shown.

The Digital Photography
Interactive Quiz Book

Test Your Knowledge and Learn Digital Photography the Fun Way

By

Ron Kness

Step 6 - Creating Your Amazon KDP Account

This is the beginning of where all of your work will start to pay off. Do it justice and take your time. The information you put in here will determine the listing of your ebook.

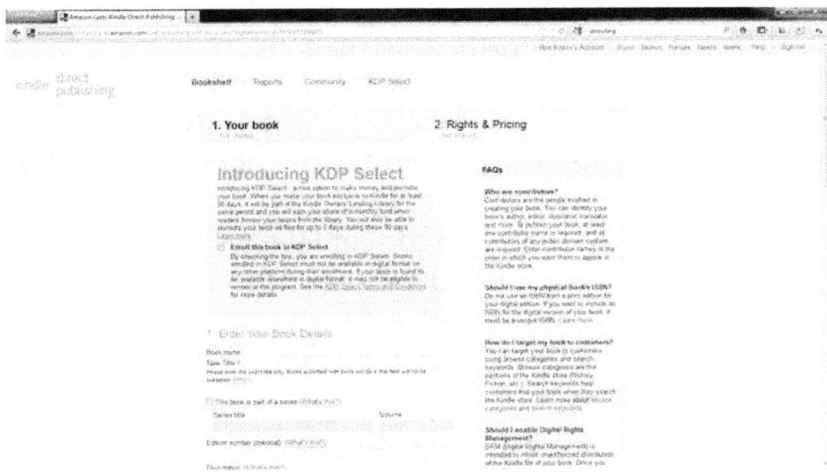

Uploading Your E-book to Amazon

1. Of course, the first step is to create an account in **Amazon's Kindle Direct Publishing**. Click on the *Sign Up* button. It is really straight-forward and free to create an account. Just follow the prompts.

2. When it comes to selecting a name, you can choose whether you want to use your real or a pen name. You can even use a female name if you are a male. Some authors do this when they feel it will improve book sales with their target readers. Or some create a gender-neutral name by using their first and middle initials along with their last name (real or pen), such a J.K. Rowling – the author of the Harry Potter series.

Enter Your Book Details

Once you have created your account, you can click on the *Add New Title* button. If you are unsure of what information to do in each part, click on the (*What's this?*) link. It will give you further instructions.

KDP Select - The first option you are faced with is whether or not you want to enroll your ebook in the KDP select program. Under this program, you commit your ebook - exclusively- to Amazon for 90 days – meaning you cannot list your book anywhere else for that time period (except in hard cover on Createspace which is a POD company owned by Amazon too). However, by enrolling your ebook in KDP Select, you can promote your ebook for free any 5 days during that 90-day period. If your readers borrow your ebook, you get a share of the monthly fund Amazon establishes for the KDP select program.

Many authors use this program by setting the price of their new ebook at $0.00 for the first five days to get some exposure and "sales". Then after the five days, they will set their actual selling price. It is a good way to generate a "buzz" about your book and earn some money initially via KDP Select.

Book Title - Next you want to enter your book title exactly as it is in your ebook and cover. If you are considering a series of books, then check the block and enter the Series Title and Volume. If not, leave blank.

Edition Number – This is a great place to enter your sub-title. If you don't have one, you can either leave it blank or enter a "1" indicating it is an original version.

Description – Take your time writing this part. Think of your description as the same type of information that would be on the inside flap of a hardcover book. After spotting your ebook by its dynamic cover, this will be the first verbiage a perspective buyer will read. This is your second "first impression", so make it good and representative of your ebook.

Book Contributors

You have to make at least one entry here, so credit yourself as the author, along with anyone else that helped you write your ebook. If you had someone draw illustrations that you used in your ebook, credit them for their work here.

You can also select what language you want your book published in here, the publication date (which can be the current date), your ISBN number, if your purchased one (but one is not required as Amazon will issue a unique ASIN to your book) and a publisher name. Being you are self-publishing, you can enter your name or your company name.

Verify Your Publishing Rights

If you did not use public domain work in your ebook, then select the second option. If you did use public domain work, then click on the *"What's this?"* button and read about securing publishing rights for public domain work.

Target Your Book to Customers

Click on the *Add Categories* button. Select two categories from the list that comes up that is representative of your ebook content. This determines where your ebook will be listed in the Kindle bookstore.

Next, select keywords that potential customers will use to search for your ebook topic. You can list up to seven keywords or keyword phrases, and while it says it is optional, use all seven keywords. You can primarily use keywords with high search values (short-tail) from the list that was generated when you were researching your book's title, but don't overlook also using a long-tail or two. You did keep that keyword list right? If not, regenerate it!

Upload Your Book Cover

Click on the *Browse for Image* button. The image they are talking about is your ebook cover saved out as either a JPEG or TIFF. If you do not have your cover ready for uploading yet, a placeholder image will be automatically inserted and you can upload your cover later.

Upload Your Book File

Generally speaking, you want to select *"Do not Enable Digital Rights Management"*. Selecting this option will allow readers to share your work and to get your name known. Then, click on the *Browse* button and select your ebook file. Once found, click the *Upload Book* button.

Previewing Your Book

Once your ebook is uploaded, you can view it in one of two ways depending on how you formatted it. If you did not use any of the formatting features of Kindle Format 8, then use the Simple Previewer. If you did use Kindle Format 8, then use the Enhanced Previewer. To download it, just click on either Windows or Mac buttons under Download Previewer. Follow onscreen instructions.

The Enhanced Previewer is also what you would use if you want to see how your ebook looks on other electronic devices, such as Kindle Fire, Kindle DX, iPhone, iPad, etc.

When previewing your e-book, you might want to consider doing the following.

• Check to make sure that all links are live and directs your readers to the desired page.

• Double-check formatting.

• Check that all images converted correctly.

If you see errors in your ebook in Preview mode, you will have to go back to your file and correct them. One handy tool to help you figure out what is wrong is the **Smashwords Style Guide**. Don't be afraid to use it to fix any stubborn formatting issues.

Set Your Publishing Territories

Most generally, you will select *Worldwide rights – all territories*, but if you only have individual rights, then select that option and select from the list the geographical rights you do have.

Set Your Royalties

You have two options – 35% or 70%. In its simplest form, if your list price of your book to be sold in the U.S. is between $2.99 and $9.99, you can choose the 70% option. However, if the list price of your book will be between $.99 and $200.00, you can use the 35% option. As you can see, for books listing between $2.99 and $9.99 either option could be used.

Before setting your price, or choosing an option, please read the next chapter on **pricing** first and the information on **Amazon's Pricing Page**, their **Terms and Conditions**.

Kindle Book Lending

If you want to expand the reach of your book and get more exposure, you might want to click on the box to allow the lending of your book. With this checked, buyers of your book can lend it to friends and family member for up to 14 days. It can be a good way to get more exposure.

Keep in mind that in the beginning, your goal is to get the word out and not about making money at this point.

Finally, read the confirmation box and click on the box if you are in compliance and agree with the statement made there. If you are ready to publish, click on the *Save and Publish* button and you are done.

If you still have more work to do before publishing, then click on the *Save as Draft* button. You can always come back later and finish it up.

Once you click on the *Save and Publish* button, your ebook should be listed on Amazon within 24 hours and usually less.

Step 7 - Pricing Your Ebook

As writers, we may not be altogether savvy about how much to charge for our ebook. And after all, isn't earning money one of the main reasons you are selling an ebook in the first place (besides getting exposure)? So, if you want to create another revenue stream, don't be bashful about pricing your ebook.

If you are writing a how-to guide to help your readers solve a problem or learn how to do something, your readers expect to pay to learn and believe it or not, most will not begrudge you the opportunity to make a little money in the process.

When establishing a price for your ebook, know that pricing is not determined completely by the actual value of a product – but rather, its *perceived* value – what readers think it is worth. So your price is actually based on what the information in your ebook is worth to your readers. It is up to you, however, to set a price that makes people think they are getting at least their value or more for the price they are paying. Keep in mind that what you put in your ebook description can go a long way to helping establish that value.

The other variable that you use to help determine your price is the royalty options.

35% Royalty Option

With this option, you can price your ebook anywhere from $0.99 to $200. This may be the option you choose if:

•   You have an exceptionally short or long e-book. Most buyers associate page count with price, so you want to follow this strategy for pricing.

•   You are planning to use an incredibly low (or even free) introductory price for marketing/exposure/ distribution reasons and then raise the price after later.

•   Your ebook cover reeks quality; your buyers know your ebook is worth at least what you are charging and probably more.

•   You know your target readers can afford to spend more than $10, based on your reader demographics.

75% Royalty Option

You can use this option if your ebook falls in the $2.99 to $9.99 range. This can be your ideal option if:

•   You plan to write and publish a series and by pricing in this range, everyone should be able to afford the entire set.

•   You know your target reader's budgets *cannot* afford to pay more than $10.

You don't have to be a rocket scientist to see that the two royalty options overlap at the $2.99 to $9.99 level. For books priced in this range, how do you determine which royalty option to choose? Use the bullets under each royalty option and choose the royalty which best matches your readership.

Step 8 - Promoting Your Ebook

As far as marketing and promotion, if your ebook delivers what the readers want from it, then some strategic and focused promoting will be all you need to get the ball rolling. As you make sales, you will see your ranking within Amazon increase.

As odd as this may sound, when promoting your e-book, don't use *paid* marketing techniques, such as pay-per-click or ads. Both of these techniques can get real expensive real quick, plus if you market correctly, you can get sales you expect using free promotion techniques.

Forum Marketing

In forum marketing, the trick is for you to establish credibility and rapport between you and your readers or you and potential affiliate marketers, fellow writers, and reviewers. So start establishing those relationships well before your ebook is released. Some forums worth exploring include:

• KindleBoards.com

• EBookGab.com

• MobileRead.com

• Kindle Forum

• Other niche-specific forums you visit.

Blog Marketing

If you already have an established blog with a decent readership base, you can use the strategies below to market your ebook:

• Post excerpts periodically before you release it to build interest in your ebook.

• Post reviews of your work written by third parties that received advanced copies of your ebook.

• Set up contests where contestants get one entry for every tweet promoting your ebook or for "Liking" your Facebook page.

• As prizes, give away copies of your ebook.

• Publish blog posts relevant to your ebook subject matter with an invitation to click on a link to get more information or to buy your ebook.

Link Exchanges

Link exchanges is basically a "I scratch your back if you'll scratch mine" type of marketing, but it can be a mutually beneficial relationship for both you and the other people. If you do any of the activities below, most likely the other person will reciprocate:

• Post a review of ebooks on a subject related to, but not directly competing with, your ebook.

• Either guest post on the other writer's blog or publish a post on your blog about the other person's ebook.

• Interview another author and make a podcast out of the interview.

- Buy the competition's ebook and they will most likely buy yours. You would be surprised how much each of you will learn from the other's ebook.

Marketing on Amazon

And don't forget about marketing yourself on Amazon itself. They have some great "exposure" tools, such as:

- *Amazon Author Page* – Once you have a KDP account, be sure to set up your Author Page. That way your readers (who are potential buyers) can get to know you better. It can be a great tool to help establish your creditability.

- *Amazon Blog* – This goes along with your Author Page. Use it to blog exclusively about your ebooks. This is also a good venue to upload trailers for your ebook.

- *Tagging* – When you upload an ebook to Amazon, you can enter up to 15 tags to improve the search of your ebook – use all 15.

Other Marketing Opportunities

Take advantage of as many of the resources below as you have time for – after all, they are free.

- *Social networking* – Facebook, LinkedIn and Pinterest

- *Instant Messaging* – Yahoo, GTalk and Skype

- *Press releases* - **Free Press Release** and **PRLog**

- *Microblogging* – Twitter and Tumbler

- *Social bookmarking* – Digg and Reddit

- *Article Directories* – Ezine, Hubpages and EHow

Don't try to start doing all of these at the same time, Start with a couple and then add in more as time permits. You will also find as you go along that some work better for you than others. Once you find those "gems", keep working them.

Conclusion

By now, you should be convinced that you can self-publish a book (whether you write it or outsource it to be written for you). Ultimately, what you say and how you say it will be what keeps people coming back for more. Listen to the feedback from your readers – they will tell you exactly how they feel. You can use that feedback for future ebooks.

If your topic is broad enough, consider self-publishing a series. You can use your current ebook to promote the next one in the series. Usually a trilogy works well, even in non-fiction (except we just call it a 3-book series).

After you have one ebook published, start working on another one, whether it is related in topic to the first one or not. Once you get the momentum started, you want to keep it going marketing what you have already published and by continually releasing new ebooks.

Follow these eight steps to self-publishing:

- Picking a topic

- Researching topic viability

- Writing

- Formatting

- Creating an ebook cover

- Creating an Amazon KDP Account

- Pricing

- Promoting

Once you have the process down and start seeing success, then just "rinse and repeat" to create more ebooks and ultimately more profits from your additional stream of revenue.

Like everything else, once you have self-published on Amazon a time or two, the process will go quicker. Good luck on your self-publishing journey!

Pillars of Gold

Five Keys to Increasing Amazon Kindle Book Sales

As I said in my first book *How to Self-Publish Your Ebook on Amazon*, getting published is a dream many of us authors have had for a long time. However up to recently, it was "out of reach" for the vast majority of us.

It meant trying to find a publishing house to pick up your book on a "book deal". Most publishing houses would not deal directly with authors, so that meant hiring an agent to represent you.

If you were lucky enough to get a book deal, you usually got a royalty advance and a small commission on each book sold – and I mean very small. And it was a long drawn-out process - it could take years before you ever saw your book for sale in a bookstore.

Then came along the Kindle e-reader from Amazon and it turned (and continues to turn) the traditional world of publishing upside down. Today, anyone can achieve "Published Author" status whether you are a writer or not. In the last book, I talked about how you can outsource the actual writing of your book if you have a good idea and want to get it published, but you are not a writer.

If you want to self-publish a book that can be read on a Kindle, publishing on Amazon - the largest online marketplace in the world- is the route to go. And it's free! No longer do you have to invest thousands of dollars up front to create and list your book that might or might not sell.

Most likely your book will not be the next bestseller (but it could be!), but self-publishing on Amazon can create a nice steady stream of passive money that doesn't take a lot of time to maintain. And I have found a synergistic energy in that as I list more books, I'm make more money. Instead of the sales of the older books dropping off, they just keep selling too.

Why Kindle?

"Why write specifically for Kindle format and not for one of the other e-reader formats?" That is a question I get asked a lot.

While you can write for other platforms, such as the epub format for Barnes and Noble's Nook and others that use the epub format, the answer is the enormous marketing and selling power of Amazon.

Amazon has over 300 million credit card numbers on file – meaning at least 300 million people have purchased something from Amazon.

Of those 300 million, people are buying *60,000* Kindle books *each and every day*. According to a recent report by an independent research group, Amazon sold $1 billion in Kindle books last year and they expect that figure to go as high as $3 billion by 2015.

In 2012, industry experts predicted Amazon will sell over 12 million new Kindle e-readers. While some of those may be Kindle users that are upgrading their old Kindle to a newer device, for many of them this will be their first Kindle – and they will need books to download so they can use it. However, many older Kindles get handed down to a child and they read a different type of books - more sales!

And the demand doesn't stop there. Don't forget to include all the other devices that can read Kindle books, such as tablets, smartphones and PCs. I think you can see why Kindle is the place to self-publish your book.

Finally, unlike going to other websites, people go to the Amazon website with one thing on their mind - the intent to buy – not just to look around.

In this book, I'm picking up where my last book *How to Self-Publish Your Ebook on Amazon* left off. I'm assuming you have already created your book and have it listed on Amazon in the Kindle marketplace. If you do not have a book listed yet, by all means start the ball rolling - if necessary, re-read the first chapter and learn how to publish on the Kindle platform.

For those that have already published a book, I'm going to show you five things you can do to optimize your Amazon book listing. For those of you not yet published, you can use this information once you have a book listed in the Kindle bookstore.

The Amazon Sales Page

Let's start with a sales page from one of my books *The Secrets of Fly Fishing for Trout.*

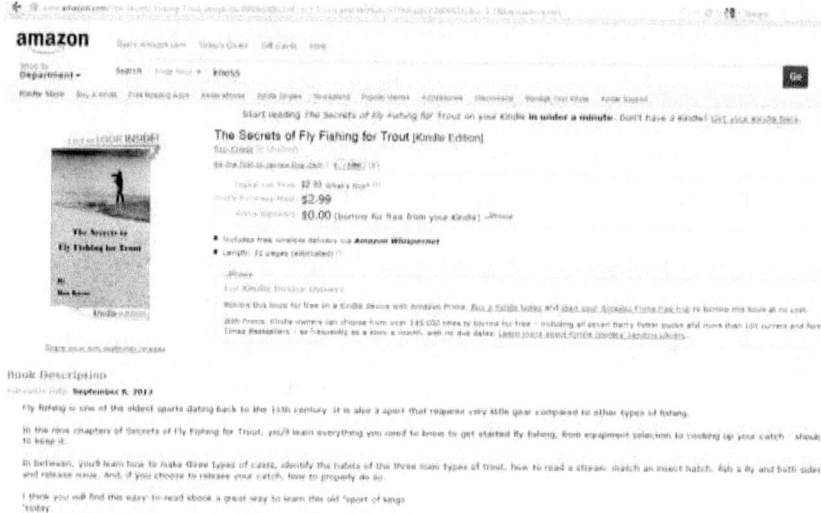

This layout is standard and representative of what you should see after entering all the information requested in the upload process and after you get your email saying your book has published.

While you can't make very many changes here, there are things you can dramatically change from another place – it is a place you probably don't even know you have. If you have published a Kindle book on Amazon, then you have an **Author Central** account. There you have the ability to make changes to your sales page that can dramatically increase your revenue from sales.

Most authors focus on creating and uploading their book, but fail to continue to improve their sales page once the book is published. Why? Because most authors don't know they can make changes to their sales page by using the free tool on Amazon's Author Central.

A book is a product and like most products, it needs a converting sales page to sell well. And yes while you will sell some books with the standard Amazon sales page, you can do so much more to increase your sales.

The 5 Pillars of Gold

There are four elements, pillars if you will, on your Amazon book sales page that affects how many books you sell. While each one in itself is important in supporting an increase in sales, together they provide a synergy of support for your book.

A fifth pillar also exists within Amazon that has an effect on sales, but it is not on the sales page – it is your marketing plan inside of Amazon itself. It, coupled with the other four pillars, are the things you can do to support the success of your book.

So, the five Pillars of Gold are a book's:

- cover

- title

- description

- pricing

- marketing plan

Cover

The cover is the most important element that draws immediate attention. A book is judged by its cover, but yet this is one of the most overlooked elements out of the five pillars. Designing an effective cover is not hard, however, if you are not graphically inclined and prefer to outsource it, we show you how to get started outsourcing in Pillar Two.

Title

With only a few seconds to capture a potential buyer's eye, there are two things that immediately catch their attention – the cover and title. In Pillar Two, we cover how to select a book title based on popular search result keywords. And if you already have a book listed, but want to change its title after reading that chapter, you can do so in your **KDP account**.

Description

Once you have the potential buyer's attention from a search results listing, and s/he has landed on your sales page, here is where the rubber meets the road. But if you leave your description as you first entered and uploaded it, you will end up with something bland and boring, and may lose sales. However, in Pillar Three, I'll show you how to use your Author Central tool to "spice" it up.

Pricing

Coming up with the "just right" price point is tricky, but we show you a method in Pillar Four to get it right so you make the maximum amount of sales.

Marketing Plan

You can just upload your book and leave the marketing to Amazon - they do a great job promoting your book – but to maximize sales, you need to work the marketing tools available to you within Amazon. In Pillar Five, we show you some things you can do – all for free – within Amazon to effectively market your book for maximum sales potential.

O.K., are you ready? Hang on! Let's go to Pillar One.

Pillar One - The Cover

Do you know how important a book cover is to a potential buyer? In a recent survey, 80% of the respondents said it matters; of that percentage, 97% said it plays a major role in whether they buy the book or not.

Because of the importance, when creating a Kindle book cover, three things must be considered. A book cover must:

- Grab the viewer's attention

- Support the book title

- Have eye-stopping visual appeal.

So, what goes into a book cover design that does these three things? Let's break each one down separately.

Grab the Viewer's Attention

After a potential buyer has selected a book from a search results list on the topic, the title is most likely the first thing that grab's his/her attention once at your sales page. However, if the potential buyer is skimming through a list of search results, a dynamic, stop-dead-in-their-tracks book cover is what will most likely draw them to your book. In this case, your title would be the second thing that captures their attention and makes them want to click on your book to learn more about it.

But, creating a stunning and effective cover is not easily achieved by many self-published authors. While you may have an eye for good writing, not everyone has an eye for good cover design. However, there are many skilled graphic designers that you can hire on places like Fiverr.com and Elance.com that can build a great cover for you for a reasonable price.

But if you have an eye for cover design, it is not that difficult to build your own cover. We discuss how to start in the next paragraph.

Support the Book Title

Three things have to tie together – the book cover, title and description. If one element is not in synch with the other two, it just doesn't work and your sales (or lack thereof) will reflect it.

An effective cover has to support the title, so that when a potential buyer is skimming through a list of books, the cover and title both are saying the same thing – one textually and the other one visually.

For example, I would not have a book title about trout fishing and then matched it with a book cover showing an image of a sunset in the desert.

The potential buyer would not expect the two to go together (and they don't) and more than likely s/he would move on and look at other books on the list. The writing in your book may be great, but if you can't get a potential buyer to stop and investigate it further, and get to him/her to read your description, you won't make the sale.

So it comes down to having the most appealing combination of typography in your title and imagery on your cover that will stop the potential buyer at your book. But we all know that people are not wired all alike, so the combination that appeals to one group of people, may not be the one that appeals to a different group.

So how do you create a cover design that addresses this challenge? The answer is to *know your target audience*.

Even before you started writing your book, you knew what kind of audience would most likely buy your book.

So, aim your book cover design at winning over your basic target audience. Think about what you knew about your target audience when you did the writing, such as:

- Are they male, female or both?

- What is their age range or age group?

- Are they new to this topic or well experienced?

- What kind of imagery would set the mood you are striving for?

- What will set your book apart from other books on the same topic?

The answers to the above questions should lead to designing visual appeal in your cover.

Have Visual Appeal

A visually appealing book cover design takes into consideration three factors that you can control:

- Clarity

- Readability

- Size

Clarity

Because cover images are so small when viewed as thumbnails, you must consider what the cover will look like at that reduced-size format. Simply put, use:

- Large fonts for the title and author's name – both must be easily readable at the thumbnail size. This means when creating your cover, go with a larger font size than you think you need.

   o If you are a new, unknown author, the title of your book should be in a larger font and placed "above the fold" - in the more prominent position at the top 1/3rd of the page.

   o Your name can be in a slightly smaller font and generally placed in the bottom 1/3rd of the page.

- A well-defined image – one with strong bright colors, but without much detail. Too much detail will not work well in the thumbnail size as the text gets lost in all the commotion going on in the image. Select a simple, but vibrant image that conveys mood, tone or topic. If the image isn't simple and clean, or if they can't discern what the image is about, they'll pass right over your book and onto the next one.

- Use contrast – make use of contrasting font color with image color. In other words, if your image color is dark, use light colored fonts and visa-versa.

Readability

If the text on your cover is unreadable, or the image indiscernible at the thumbnail size, your potential buyer will most likely slide right past your book and not buy. If your cover will not stop the potential buyer in the few precious seconds you have before that person moves on, then it is not an effective cover for your book. Both the image and text must be clear, crisp and most importantly, readable at the thumbnail size.

Size

When sizing your cover for the Kindle platform, you want the long side to be at least 1,000 pixels high. You also want to keep a 1.6 height/width ratio, meaning the width for a 1,000 pixel high image would be 600 pixels. However, Amazon will let you go as high as 2,500 pixels (with the width at 1,500 pixels.)

Pillar One - The Title

What are the two main things you see when you look at the sales page below?

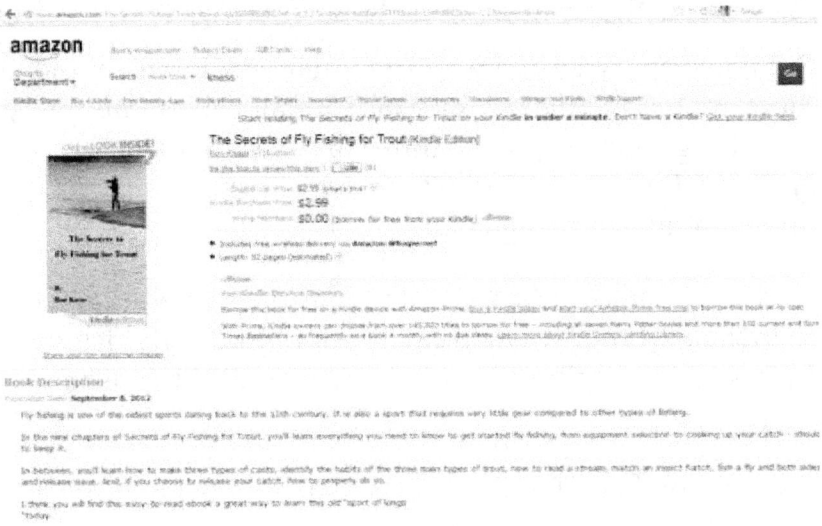

The book title and cover of course. You will probably look at the book cover first because you arrived here by clicking on the book title from an Amazon search on the topic in the beginning But the real question is why did you click on this particular title and not one of the other titles listed?

That's right, the words in the title. As an author and/or publisher, by selecting the right words for your title, you build up a curiosity in the perspective buyer that forces s/he to click on your title out of a list to see more. You can't sell a book unless you get them to the sales page, so creating a title is a very important first step.

When creating a title, your goal is to create a curiosity and you do that by choosing relative keywords in your title that targets a certain segment of your market.

For example, I could have chosen the titles of *The Secrets of Fly Fishing* or *The Secrets of Fishing for Trout*.

But those are two separate target markets. For example, there are many other species of fish that can be caught by fly fishing, such as pike, panfish and bass, so *The Secrets of Fly Fishing* really doesn't work as I'm specifically talking about catching trout.

And *The Secrets of Fishing for Trout* doesn't work either as there are other ways to catch trout besides fly fishing, such as with a spin-cast rod and reel and with live bait verses artificial flies.

Because my book focuses on just catching trout with a fly rod and reel, my target market are trout fishermen who catch trout by fly fishing. See the difference and how those keywords of *trout* and *fly fishing* pertain to my narrowed target market?

When searching for keywords, you can use Amazon's search feature itself to help you. For example when I enter the words fly fishing, the first word in the list it brings up is fly fishing. If I search using the word *trout*, trout is the first word. So it would make sense to create a title using both keyword /keyword phrases, which is why my title has both fly fishing and trout – both are strong keywords in Amazon for my target market.

You can also use Google's free keyword tool.

It is a great tool to use when you want to create a large list of keywords around a particular topic. It also includes several "long-tail" keywords, keywords that have a smaller number of searches, but are still viable keywords that you may want to use in your title, depending on the topic or your book.

If you are marketing your book world-wide, use the Global Monthly Search data. If you are limiting your book to just one area, then change the country and language in the *Advanced Options and Filters*, and use the Local Monthly Search data as it will be more accurate to your particular area.

If I enter the words "fly fishing", I see that keyword gets 1,000,000 global searches per month at this time of writing.

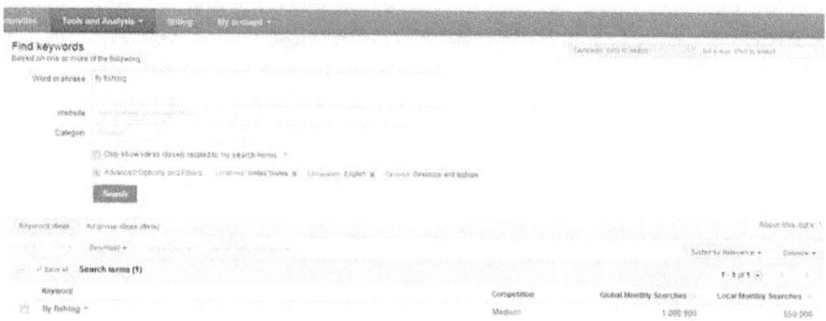

If I enter the word "trout", it brings up 1,830,000 global monthly searches, indicating both trout and fly fishing are heavily searched keywords.

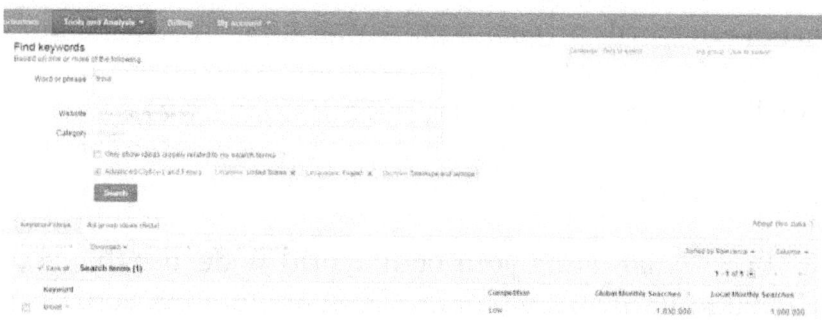

Along with keywords, there are many popular phrases that can be successfully used in a title along with relevant keywords, such as:

- The Secret to _____

- [insert number] Secrets to _____

- Top [insert number] Ways to _____

- Top [insert number] Reasons to _____

- Everything You Ever Wanted to Know About _____

- _____ - Things to Consider

- Little Known Ways to _____

- [insert number] Crucial Steps to _____

- [insert number] Mistakes to Avoid When _____

- How to _____ in [insert number] Easy Steps

- How to _____ Even if _____

- _____ - Do It Right the First Time

- How to Get Your _____ Back on Track

- How to Get _____ in Less Than [insert time period]

These are only a few of the popular ones as the list goes on and on. So after doing some keyword research both in Amazon and Google, I settled on the title of *The Secrets of Fly Fishing for Trout.*

If you are already published and after reading this chapter, you decide you would like to change your book title, you can go to your KDP account and make the change.

First, select the book you want to change by checking the box to the left of your book title. Then click on the *Actions* button on either the top or bottom left.

Select *Edit Book Details* from the drop-down menu. Then change your book title and then click on the *Save and Continue* button at the bottom of the page.

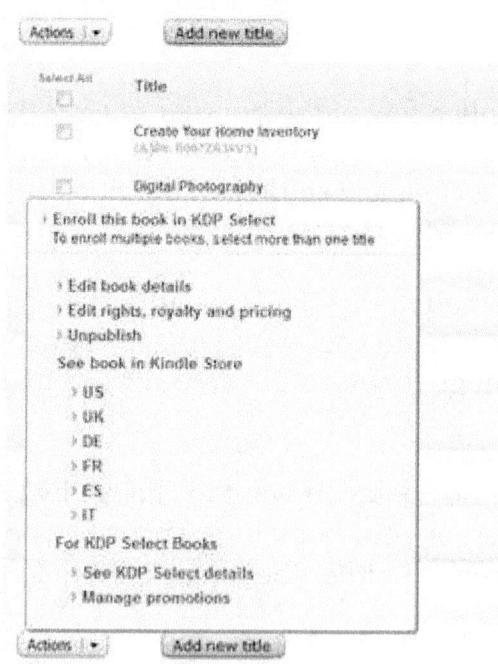

Pillar Three - The Description

After your book title and cover, the most important pillar is your book description. Once the potential buyer has gotten past these two objects, your description is what will close the sale.

When creating your description, be sure to answer these potential buyer's questions:

• What is the book about?

• Will it solve my problem?

• Will it deliver what the cover and title promised?

• Is the level of writing in the description representative of the writing in the book?

If you answer these questions, you have a good chance at keeping the person on your sales page and maybe even converting him/her into a buyer.

When writing your description, focus on the features *and* benefits. In other words, what will your book do for the buyer? If that is not clear, you most likely lost a sale.

Be sure to include any accolades you may have gotten along with at least one good review if you have any yet. If not, you can add these things in later as you receive them. Address any final questions your potential buyer may have such as "Is this book right for me?" Finally, be sure to wrap up your description with a call to action – a compelling reason for the person to buy.

When you first write your description, you can include all of these things, but it is almost impossible to create a good looking layout because initially you do not have bolding, bulleting, italics and other formatting features available to you.

To give you an example, below is my original description as I had entered it when I first uploaded my book and created my book's sales page:

"Fly fishing is one of the oldest sports dating back to the 15th century. It is also a sport that requires very little gear compared to other types of fishing.

In the nine chapters of Secrets of Fly Fishing for Trout, you'll learn everything you need to know to get started fly fishing, from equipment selection to cooking up your catch - should you decide to keep it.

In between, you'll learn how to make three types of casts, identify the habits of the three main types of trout, how to read a stream, match an insect hatch, fish a fly and both sides of the catch and release issue. And, if you choose to release your catch, how to properly do so.

I think you will find this easy-to-read ebook a great way to learn this old "sport of kings" today".

As you can see, it was pretty much just text with no formatting. Now this is what it looks like after editing it in Author Central:

"Fly fishing is one of the oldest sports dating back to the 15th century. It is also a sport that requires very little gear compared to other types of fishing.

What Do You Get?

Chapters include:

* "Introduction" – A look at the old "sport of kings".

* "Choosing Fly-Fishing Equipment Right for You" – Like any other sport, having the right equipment makes the sport more enjoyable.

* "Casting for Success" – Learn three casting moves in an hour to start fly-fishing

* "Three Main Types of Trout" – Learn about the habitat, range, coloration and feeding habits of the three main species of trout.

* "Reading Stream Habitat" – Increase your chances of success by learning to identify where trout prefer to hang out.

* "Replicating the Hatch? – How to identify and choose what trout are currently eating.

* "Work It Baby, Work It" – Correctly present a fishing fly or go home empty-handed.

* "To Release or Not Release, That Is the Question" – A discussion on both sides of this issue and why at times it is better to keep a fish or two.

* "Cleaning and Preparing Trout for Cooking and Smoking" – Preparation is the key to a great tasting meal and it starts the minute you keep the fish.

The Bottom Line Benefit

How will this book benefit you? If you have always wanted to learn how to fly-fish, then this book is for you. We start at the beginning and logically discuss each chapter – the next one building on the previous one.

Once you have finished the book, you will have a fundamental understanding of how practice the "Sport of Kings" and end up with a tasty meat on your table, if you choose to keep your catch.

To learn how to fly fish, get the easy read The Secrets of Fly Fishing for Trout right now."

Do you notice the upgraded visual appeal factor in the new version? To me it is odd why you can't do this right away when building your book sales page instead of having to do it after the fact, but that is the way Amazon is currently set-up.

Pillar Four - Pricing

When it comes to pricing, picking the correct price is more of an art than science. And most likely, it will take some testing before you connect on the proper price.

Establishing a price for your book is based more on its *perceived value* – what readers think it is worth - rather than its actual worth. So while you can select your initial pricing of your book, your customers will dictate its final price.

Initially, set a price where you think buyers will get value for the money they paid for your book. But after setting your initial price, you will have to monitor your sales and Amazon ranking. As both increase, slowly increase the price of your book (ranging from $0.50 to $1.00) every few days to a week.

At some point sales will level out and you know you have your price about right. But over time though, sales will start to drop. Then you want to start dropping your price until sales stabilize out again.

The other variable to help you determine your price (at least initially) are the royalty options. Amazon has two.

35% Royalty Option

With this option, you can price your book anywhere from $0.99 to $200. This may be your best option if:

• Your book is exceptionally short or long (or a large file size). Most buyers associate page count with price, so you may want to follow this strategy for pricing.

- You are planning to price your book at a $0.99 introductory price for exposure purposes and then raise your price later.

- You know your target readers can afford to pay more than $10, if you plan on your price being over that amount.

70% Royalty Option

If your book falls in the $2.99 to $9.99 range, this may be your ideal option if:

- You plan to write and publish a series and by pricing in this range, everyone should be able to afford the entire set.

- You know your target reader's budgets cannot afford to pay more than $10. You must also have you book enrolled in KDP Select to use this option.

Note: Under the 70% option, Amazon charges you for delivery costs at the rate of $0.15 per MB. Even small book files will cost you $0.01 for them to deliver it digitally. While it does not sound like much, it can add up over time and subtract from your overall bottom line.

You may have noticed right away that the two options overlap at the $2.99 to $9.99 level. For books priced in this range, how do you determine which royalty option to choose? Use the bullets under each royalty option and choose the royalty which best matches your readership and that will provide you the most money in your pocket.

Pillar Five - The Amazon Marketing Plan

Within Amazon itself, there are a few things you can do to get some additional exposure and increase your potential for sales:

•   *Amazon Author Page* – Once you have an __Author Central__ account, be sure to set up your biography located under the Profile Tab. This is a great way to show your viewers who you are and what you do. It is a great first step toward establishing the trust factor with your readers (who are potential buyers) and it is also a great tool you can use to establish your creditability, i.e., why you are qualified to write a book on this particular topic.

•   *Author Central Blog* – Also under the Profile Tab on your Author Page is a place where you can enter a link to your blog feed. If you don't already have a blog set up where you can talk about your books, create one and put the link to it in your Author Central Blog.

As far as what to blog about, talk exclusively about your book(s). How you come up with the title, cover, topic, etc. This is also a good venue to upload information similar to what a reader will find in the "Look Inside" feature of your book listing.

•   *Amazon Associate's Store (Astore)*

Once you have some books listed in the Kindle Marketplace, set up an Astore and list your books as a page on your website. The advantage is if you list your Astore affiliate link on your website, not only do you get your normal royalty percentage from Amazon for each book that sells, you get an additional 8.5% percent when they buy through your Astore affiliate link. Below is my Astore page for my Kindle books.

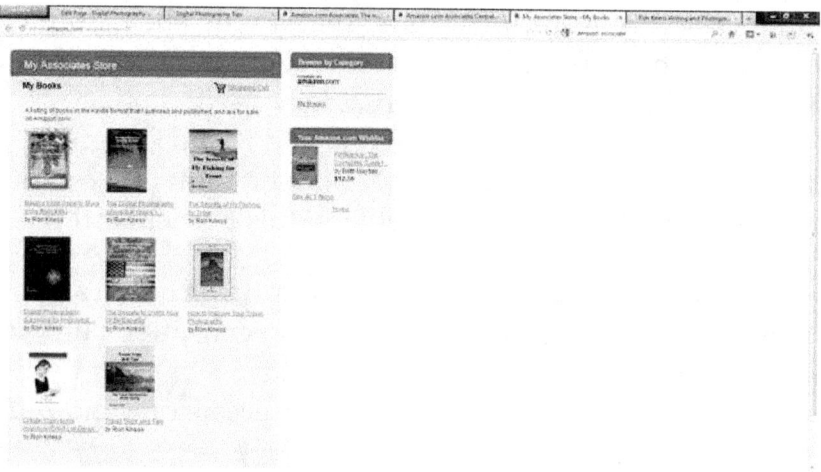

Tagging – When you upload a Kindle book to Amazon, there is a place where you can enter up to 15 tags to improve the search ranking of your book – use all 15. Think about what a potential buyer would enter into the Search box on Amazon.com if s/he were looking for a book on your topic. Those are the keywords/keyword phrases you should enter as tags.

Keyword Consistency - Make sure you use many of the same keywords on your Author Central page, personal website/blog and in your book description. By using the same words in all three places, you are optimizing search engine results for your book. Also linking is important; include links both to and from your Amazon Central page and to and from your personal website/blog.

KDP Select - Another popular marketing strategy many authors are using is to enter their books into the KDP Select marketing program. By enrolling in KDP Select, you can:

- Reach an expanded and different audience through the Lending Program.

- Earn more royalties as you get a royalty off each book lent out from the Owners Lending Library.

- Promote your book as free for up to five days out of each 90-day KDP Select period.

Note: While you have your book listed in KDP Select, it cannot be listed anywhere else in the digital format, however, you can sell it as a physically printed book. At the end of your initial 90-day period, you have the option to renew your KDP Select agreement or let it expire. Once expired, you are free to list your book on other places besides Amazon.

Perceived Value – Early in the morning on the first day of your "free" day, increase the price of your free book in your listing. That way when people "buy" your free book, they can see how much they are saving. Once your free days are over, then lower your price again.

knessr@gmail.com

Getting the Most from Free

To get the maximum visibility and exposure for your book, use your free period to your advantage by spreading the word outside Amazon that people can "buy" and download your book for free on certain days.

Two to three weeks before your "free" days begin, submit your information to the following sites which can promote you and your book to their networks:

DIGITAL BOOK TODAY

KINDLE BOARDS –> The Book Bazaar

PIXEL OF INK

KINDLE AUTHOR

BARGAIN EBOOK HUNTER

EREADERNEWSTODAY

STORYFINDS

FREEBOOKSDAILY

FREEBOOKSY

KINDLEBOOKPROMOS

CENTSIBLEEREADS

On the day first free day, Tweet out your message on Twitter at the following sites:

@DigitalBkToday @kindleebooks @Kindlestuff @KindleBookKing @KindleFreeBook @free_kindle @FreeReadFeed @4FreeKindleBook @KindleFreeBooks @KindleFreeStuff @KindleSurprise @FreeKindleStuff @KindleUpdates @freebookpromos @freebooksy @Kindlbookreview @Kindlefreebies @KindleUK @Kindle_Max @KindleBlaze @KindleBookBlast

Don't forget to send out tweets to these hashtags:

#kindle #kindlefire #ebooks #ebook #freeebook #Kindlefreebooks #Kindledeals #FREE #mustread #goodreads #greatreads #freebie #freebies #kindlebook

In your tweets, ask people to retweet your message. Finally, post to your Facebook, LinkedIn and Pinterest account, along with sending out an email to your mailing list (if you have one yet), and uploading a post to your blog about your book being free for downloading during specified days.

While there is some controversy about the effectiveness of social marketing unless you are a well-known author with thousands of followers, it is my belief that you'll get some benefit by spreading your word far and wide. Even if you only get a few book sales out of it, it would be worth it.

Conclusion

As with the selling of any product, marketing is the decisive factor whether something sells well or not. The best product will fail without an effective marketing plan as well as a poor product will sell good with a great marketing plan. As the old saying goes, with your marketing plan, you should be able to "sell refrigerators to Eskimos."

In this book we covered how to effectively market your ebook by creating an effective:

- title

- book cover

- description

- along with a discussion on some pricing strategies and using some marketing tools found within Amazon.

One of the great things with having a book listing in Amazon is that you can change it as often as you like. However, note that when you do make certain changes, it can take up to 12 hours before those changes take effect.

In my next book - *Kindle Advanced Strategies* - I'll show you some more creative ways you can make your description even better, but it requires some knowledge of working with HTML tags. We'll show you how to:

- bold

- center

- center and bold

- italics

- center and italics

- make a bulleted list

- make a numbered list

- use H1 through H6 headlining

- headline and center

- add photos.

And yes you can do some of these things in Author Central, but you can do so much more once you know how use Amazon's HTML (and it is different than "normal" HTML).

I will also get more into the outsourcing process if you want to hire a writer for a reasonable price to actually write your book for you.

In the book you are reading now, I wanted to keep things simple – I wanted to explain things that anyone could do to improve book sales regardless of their level of skill with computers.

I hope you have gained some knowledge from this book on how you can increase your potential to make more sales from your Kindle-listed book by working with your book's:

- title

- cover

- description

- pricing

- marketing.

Please keep coming back to my *Amazon Author Page* to see what new books I have recently listed.

Kindle Advanced Strategies

- -

Taking It to the Next Level

Welcome to *Kindle Advance Strategies – Taking It to the Next Level*. This is the third book in my series *Writing for the Kindle Market.*

In the first book, *How to Self-Publish Your Ebook on Amazon - The Nuts and Bolts, Step-by-Step Guide to Self-Publishing Freedom*, I focused on:

- Picking a topic

- Writing and formatting

- Creating an ebook cover

- Setting Up a KDP Account

- Pricing

- Promoting

In my second book, *Pillars of Gold - Five Keys to Increasing Amazon Kindle Book Sales*, my focus was on changing your book listing information or if you had not published a book yet, the things to think about before you publish, such as:

- Title Page

- Legal Information/Disclaimers

- Introduction

- Sales Page

- The Five Pillars of Gold

  o Title

  o Cover

  o Description

  o Pricing

  o Marketing

In this latest book in the series, I focus on:

- Rewriting your book description using Amazon's unique HTML coding system.

- How to write picture books in a hot niche.

- How to outsource your Kindle writing, if you do not want or can't write your book yourself.

Each book builds on the previous one, so if you have not read the first two yet, I suggest you do. So without further ado, let's get to it!

Coding Amazon's Sales Page Description

There are three things that will stop a person at your book listing instead of someone else's book listing. The first two are your title and book cover. The third one is your book description.

As I described in my last book *Pillars of Gold*, you can go into your Author's Page at Author Central and edit your description once your book has published. While the edit feature there allows you to do some basic formatting, such as bolding, italics, and both bulleted and numbered lists, you can't do such things as centering, centering and bolding, centering and italics, H1 through H6 headlining, headlining and centering, or adding photos.

However, by knowing Amazon's HTML coding, you can do these things and more. Just be sure you are in the *EDIT HTML* tab and not the *COMPOSE* Tab before starting to code your book description.

Amazon uses a different HTML code that at first looks very confusing – but really it isn't. If you are familiar with standard HTML coding, then you are familiar with the "<" and ">" tags.

Instead of using less-than (<) and greater-than (>) tags, Amazon replaces these tags with the "<" and ">" tags respectively (without the quotes). So instead of coding Kindle in italics by using <i>Kindle</i>, it would read <i>Kindle</i> instead.

If you are going to use italics once in your description, then you can just code it out as I did above using Amazon's HTML, however, if you have several instances of the same code, you may want to code it out once, using normal HTML, and then replace it with Amazon HTML by using your word processing program's Find and Replace feature.

So <i>Kindle</i> would become <i>Kindle</i> by finding <i> and replacing it with <i> and </i> and replacing it with </i> .

Here is the coding for many of the formatting features you can use in your book's description:

Action	Amazon HTML Code
Result	

Bold   <b>KINDLE</b>
KINDLE

Italics   <i>KINDLE</i>
KINDLE

Center   <center>KINDLE</center>

KINDLE

Center and Bold
<center><b>KINDLE</center></b>

KINDLE

Center and Italics
<center><i>KINDLE</center></i>

KINDLE

Make a bulleted list

<ul>

<li>KINDLE1</li>

<li>KINDLE2</li>

<li>KINDLE3</li>

</ul>

Appears as:

- KINDLE

- KINDLE

- KINDLE

Make a numbered list

<ol>

<li>KINDLE1</li>

<li>KINDLE2</li>

<li>KINDLE3</li>

</ol>

Appears as:

1. KINDLE

2. KINDLE

3.   KINDLE

H1 Headlining   <h1>KINDLE</h1>

KINDLE

H2 Headlining   <h2>KINDLE</h2>

Kindle

Notice the H2 string shows up as Amazon orange as far as the font color.

Use the same string of code for H3 through H6. Just change the numbers in the string.

Headline and center
<center><h1>KINDLE</h1></center>

Kindle

If you can rewire your brain to think of "<" as "<" and" >" as ">", you'll do just fine with Amazon HTML coding. The rest of the HTML coding is pretty much the same as normal coding.

Otherwise, you could hire a coder to do the work for you for around $35 to $50 per hour. It would take about a half hour to code a book description page.

Adding photos

As far as adding photos, Amazon doesn't allow you to upload photos directly into your description. Instead, you first have to upload your photo to a website and then add in the url of the photo.

So the code to add an image looks like this: <img src="the full url of your photo here" align="left" />. This time leave in the quotes on each end of your url.

By applying the HTML changes to your description, you can go from the standard listing like this:

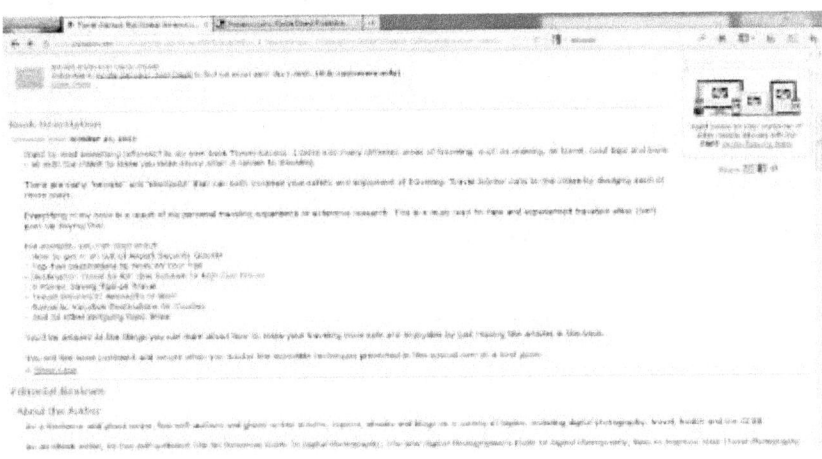

To the one like this:

Notice this enhanced book description has:

- a cover image

- text centering

- gold text headlining - a result of the H2 command in Amazon HTML coding.

None of these things can be done using the regular edit features in Author Central.

One Hot Niche . . . And Just in Time

To show you just how hot this niche really is, in January 2011, it sold $3.9 million dollars in ebooks. Just one year later – in January 2012 – sales increased 475.1%, up to $22.6 million for just one month. How big a piece of this pie would you like?

Now that I have your attention, I'll reveal the niche – digital children picture books.

Why does this niche sell so well?

The reasons are many, including:

•   **Popularity.** As Kindle popularity increases, parents are either buying (or handing down older model) Kindles to their children.

•   **Familiarity.** Parents are already familiar with using a Kindle to read for themselves, so it is natural to read a book to a child on one.

•   **Convenience.** It is easy and fast to order and receive a Kindle book within minutes. No more leaving the house and driving to the bookstore.

•   **Price.** Most Kindle books are far cheaper to buy than hardcover books.

Topics

Another reason for the popularity of children picture Kindle books are the large number of categories and age ranges. For example, some popular themes that would pertain to 4 to 8 year-olds might be:

- Vocabulary.

- Lessons/social behavior.

- Bedtime.

- Fairy Tales.

- Dealing with Fears/situations.

- Rhyming.

- ABC's.

- Humor/gross.

- Animals.

As expected, ebooks aimed at the younger children will have more pictures/illustrations than text while the ebooks for the older children will have more text and less pictures/illustrations.

Designing the Ebook

To start with, try to select a topic broad enough that you can create an ebook length that is at least 15 to 20 pages. Start out by storyboarding your ebook on a pad of paper. Draw out crude versions of your pictures or illustrations that you want in the book and fill in the text as required.

Once you have your storyline drawn up, create the artwork. You have three options here:

• Draw/photograph it yourself.

• Outsource it.

• Use a combination of both.

Creating the Ebook

There are basically two methods you can use. The first method only requires an image editor and word processing program, such as Microsoft word.

Method One

If you are using Microsoft Word, open up a new document and select Page Layout from the topline menu. Click on **MARGINS** and select the **Custom Margins** and set your paper size in the Paper tab to 5.39" for width and 7.91" for height. Click on the **OK** button.

Enter your text and insert your pictures/illustrations (now referred to as images) in the appropriate places. Make your chapter heading as Heading 1 just as you would do in any other ebook you would make. Create your Table of Contents.

Click on an image. From the **Picture Tools** menu, click on **Format** and then **Compress Pictures**.

Make sure the **Compress Options** are unchecked and check the resolution setting of Screen 150ppi. Click the **OK** button.

If you have an ebook heavily laden with images, you want to compress them so that your final ebook file size will be as small as possible. Why? Because Amazon charges you a delivery fee for each ebook sold and if your ebook is over 1MB in size, you pay more for each book sold.

Method Two

This method takes more work in the beginning, but less work to put it together as this style ebook is all images. First create your images using a versatile image-editing program. You want a program that will let you do creative things, such as:

- Add colorful backgrounds.

- Use fancy text fonts.

- Make your first letters of your text in a larger font.

- Use fancy borders.

While not really considered an image-editing program, one of my favorites is Microsoft Publisher. Save your work out as 7.5" X 10.15" (540 X 731 pixels) JPEGs.

Set up your document as in Method one and insert your images. Finish out your document as you would in Method One.

If you are just starting out creating ebooks, Method one is the simpler one to use.

With either method, finish out your ebook by saving it out as a Web Filtered document. This will create an HTML file.

Then open your HTML document in the Kindle Previewer and let the software convert your document to a .mobi file. View the resulting MOBI file on Kindle Previewer to ensure everything converted correctly.

What is neat about these picture book methods is that they are not limited to just the children's market. You could also create a Kindle picture, coffee-table style book on many different topics using this same method. Travel and How-to are two topics that would make great Kindle picture books. You are only limited by your imagination!

Outsourcing

When you're writing job description, there are some things you can do differently from the others that will make your job descriptions stand out in the crowd. Not only will these things get you better quality bids, but you will get a higher quality of candidates submitting bids.

Red Cow or Purple Ninja?

One of the issues with bids submitted in response to your job posting is that some people submit a bid on every job listed without really reading the job posting. So to separate those really serious about doing the job from the mass posters, I include an absurd two-word phrase that I tell them has to be at the beginning of their bid. If it isn't there, I move on to the next bid. You can use phrases such as "Purple Ninja", "Red Cow", etc. Make it something that would not naturally occur in a bid.

In my job posting, I say, "*At the top of your bid, make sure to have the words "Purple Ninja"* (or whatever phrase I'm using at the time). I love this strategy because many people don't even bother to read the job descriptions thoroughly. They just see a job and apply for it.

My problem with that is I like to work with detail-oriented people and if they aren't detail oriented enough to read the full description before they submit a bid, I don't want them working for me. So if you put in your job description, "*Make sure these words are in your bid,*" and then they aren't, eliminate them from consideration because they obviously can't follow simple directions.

If they have included my words in their response, great – they have made it over the first elimination hurdle. But what you will find with this strategy is it will eliminate around 70% of the applicants. It will save you a lot of time reading through bids that most likely would not have worked out anyway.

Next, you always want to include a very specific timeline in your job description. For example write something like *"I need a 20-page draft document written and to me within seven days,"* or *"I need this book written and to me no later than December 10th."*

However you write it, be very specific. This does two things; first, if someone can't meet your timeline, they most likely won't bid. And two, it gives the person bidding a specific date or timeline up front, so they know when the project has to be done. If you do end up accepting their bid, you have a specific date that you can hold them to. If they don't meet the deadline, you can reflect it accordingly in the feedback you post about how they did your work.

By including a specific date, I as the requestor can then hold the provider accountable. If you don't specify a completion date, then you can't hold them accountable that particular element of the job, although there are other things you can hold them accountable for.

Ask for a sample of their writing preferably in the niche of your job, but it doesn't have to be in that niche. You are looking to see if they have a writing "voice" similar to yours and something so you can assess the quality of their work.

Also, if their writing does not end up being written similarly to their sample, you can question if their sample was really written by them or someone else. If the requestor is not willing to send you a sample of their writing, then maybe they are not the person for the job.

In your job description, mention the fact that you will leave them **extraordinary positive feedback** if they do a good job - that's really important to people submitting bids. A lot of freelancers on these job sites are judged by their feedback, so really good feedback makes them look really, really good and can lead to them getting more jobs based on their feedback.

Besides all the other information in a posting, these are things you want to include in every job description. Let the potential candidates know why this job is better than other ones listed.

Below are a couple of job posting samples that you can use as is or modify to your requirements.

Craigslist Job Posting Format Example

"Subject: Need long term freelancers for steady work.

I need to hire a person who likes to write.

This job would be perfect for someone needing a little extra cash, such as a student, stay at home parent, someone unemployed, etc.

Each writing piece will be on [Insert your topic here] and at least 500 words long. You do a great job on this assignment; you will have an opportunity to write on many other different topics.

This is pretty easy work because:

a) The articles don't need a lot of research - just an intro, a few main points about the topic and a conclusion.

b) I will give you researched material so you can probably write an article in 10 minutes after you have written a few of them.

However, just so you know, your first article may take up to 30 minutes and your second article 20 minutes before you get the process down to 10 minutes.

You will work as a freelance contractor for me and we will provide you with a 1099 at the end of each financial year.

If you are interested, please contact [insert your email here if the job site will allow it – some don't] or reply back with a bid. Be sure and have the words "Red Cow" in the email subject line or at the beginning of your bid. All job posting responses without "Red Cow" will be eliminated.

Thank you for applying and if selected to work for me, we're looking forward to a mutually beneficial working arrangement.

Sincerely,

[Insert your name]

P.S. F.A.Q. (Note: By inserting FAQs, it makes it look as if we've gotten a ton of responses to this job posting.)

Q: Where do these articles go?

A: They will be primarily used in websites and newsletters.

Q: Do I get credit for my articles?

A: You will be writing these articles on a work-for-hire basis, so you will NOT get credit.

Q: Can I use you as a reference for other jobs I may be applying for in the future?

A: Absolutely, as long as you do a good job.

Q: How many articles do I need to write per week?

A: You tell us how many you're comfortable writing. We expect all article assignments to be completed within 5 days, so let us know how many you can do per week and we will make sure to never assign you more than that.

Q: How will I get paid?

A: We pay every Sunday for all the articles you have done that week via PayPal. If you do not have an account yet, please set one up. It's completely legitimate and you can transfer your pay directly into your bank account."

Kindle Book Job Posting Example

"Subject: Native English Writer Needed To Write a Kindle Book

I am looking for a GREAT NATIVE ENGLISH-SPEAKING WRITER who can write a detailed book in Kindle format on **[Enter Subject Here]** *and finish it by the deadline of* **[Enter Completion Date Here]**.

If you do a great job, I'll reward you with EXTRAORDINARY positive feedback as well as hire you for other jobs.

This project needs to be written in a conversational yet informative tone by someone who has an excellent grasp of the English language (preferably a native English writer, unless you are PHENOMENAL at writing in English).

The book will be approximately [Enter number of words or pages]. I can either provide you with an outline or you can create one on what you think should be in the book and have me review it first so that we're both on the same page.

Please bid on how much you expect to receive to write this project. Put down whatever amount you want, but know that price is a big factor here as to whether you get the project or not.

Be sure to mention "Red Ninja"[or whatever phrase you use] at the beginning of bid, so I know you are a detailed-oriented person that can follow instructions.

In your bid, also tell me how long it would take you to complete. Ideally, I would love this back on [Enter your deadline]. If that is not possible, we might be able to negotiate an acceptable date for both of us, however though, I will give a higher priority to those who can meet the deadline.

Also, please include a sample article on [Enter your Niche Here]. If you do not have a sample on this niche, submit a sample article on anything.

Finally, thank-you in advance for your bid. We will take it under consideration and let you know if we select you.

[Enter Your Name Here]"

These are just a couple of samples, but the all the necessary structure is in both of these examples. You can tailor them to your individual needs. Now onto some of the places where you can post your job descriptions.

Outsourcing Job Sites

There are many, many sites where you can post writing jobs. I showcased three that I have successfully used in the past. They are:

- Elance.com

- Craigslist.org

- Freelancer.com

Elance.com

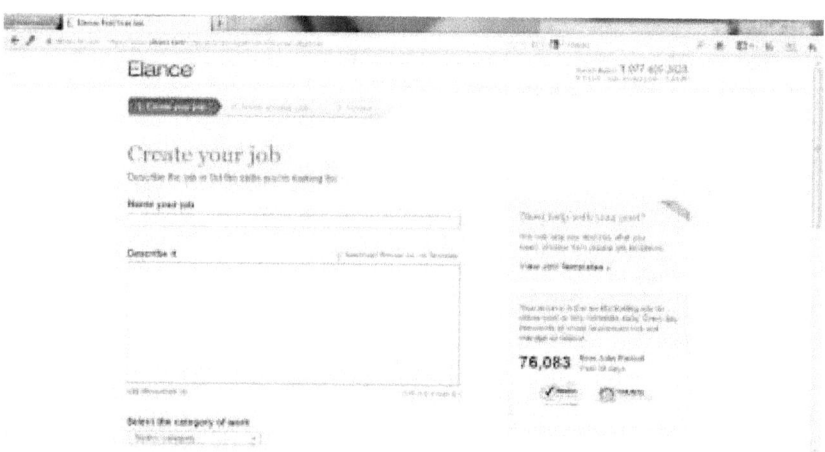

If you have not created an account before in Elance, you will have to do that first. Then click on "I Want to Hire". The form above will come up where you can enter your job information.

First enter the name of your job and the description keeping in mind the information in the last chapter for your description information.

Next select the category of work from the drop-down box, such as *Writing and Translation*. You can then select a subcategory, such as *Ebooks*. If you have some specific skills you want, you can select these as well from the next drop-down box.

Now select whether your job is an hourly rate or a fixed price. Depending on which one you select, the budget drop-down box will change and you can select the range you are willing to pay, or you can enter in custom information.

Next under the *Privacy and Other Option* area, you can select one of the options for *Job Location, Posting Length in Days, Proposed Start Date, Job Posting Visibility* and finally checking the *1099 Tax Filing Box* or leaving it blank.

Then either click on *Continue* or *Save & Post Later* button and you are done.

Craigslist.org

Click on the *U.S.* button. Then select which state and city or closest city you are located. Click on *Gigs* and then *Writing*. Now in the upper right-hand corner of your screen, click on *Post*.

Click the radio button "I want to hire someone" and then click *Continue*. Next choose a category, such as writing gigs. Next choose your area.

Now enter your *Posting Title, Specific Location* and *Reply To* email address.

Enter your job description. Click on the *Pay* radio button and be as descriptive as possible. Now click on the *Continue* button. You're done!

Freelancer.com

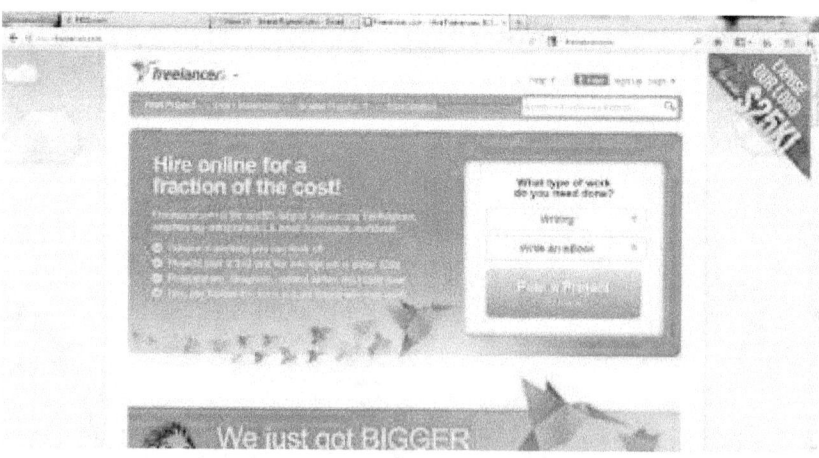

Click the *Sign Up* button in the upper right-hand corner. Once signed up and logged in, click on the orange *Post Project* button on the right side of your screen.

Enter a *Project Name* and then the category of work you require from the drop-down box. You also have an opportunity to select a sub-category.

Next, you can select up to three skills you want in the person you hire.

Describe your project in great detail. *Select Project Type* and as to whether it is a fixed price or hourly job. Finally select a *Budget Range*.

If you want to further promote your job posting, you can select any of the options under *Promote Your Listing*.

If you do not want any of the options, then skip down to and click on the *Post Project Now* button. You project will be reviewed by a Freelancer.com Staff Member before it goes live.

Conclusion

In this Kindle book, we discussed how to:

- Code a book description page using Amazon HTML coding

- Create children picture books

- Outsource writing

- Post job descriptions.

While this is slated to be the last book in my Writing for the Kindle Market series, things are constantly changing; if enough new information becomes available or the existing information drastically changes, I'll write a fourth book in the series just to keep you abreast of what is happening with writing Kindle books.

As I said in my Introduction, if you have not yet read the first two books in this book, I encourage you to do so. In the first book, *How to Self-Publish Your Ebook on Amazon - The Nuts and Bolts, Step-by-Step Guide to Self-Publishing Freedom*, I focused on:

- Picking a topic

- Writing and formatting

- Creating an ebook cover

- Setting Up a KDP Account

- Pricing

- Promoting

In my second book, *Pillars of Gold - Five Keys to Increasing Amazon Kindle Book Sales*, my focus was on changing your book listing information or if you had not published a book yet, the things to think of before you publish, such as:

- Title Page

- Legal Information/Disclaimers

- Introduction

- Sales Page

- The Five Pillars of Gold

    o   Title

    o   Cover

    o   Description

    o   Pricing

    o   Marketing

Each book builds on the prior one(s), so to get the whole picture, you have to read all three of them.

And finally please keep coming back to my Amazon Author Page to see what new books I have recently listed. Happy writing!

Legal Information

appropriately qualified professional before making any business decision.

The contributor does not accept any responsibility for any liabilities resulting from the business decisions made by purchasers of this book. Any perceived slights of specific people, products, services or organizations are completely unintentional.

RELEASE FROM LIABILITY:

No formal product support is provided. In no event will the author of this product, any distributors or affiliates be liable to any party for any direct, indirect, special, incidental, punitive or other consequential damages arising directly or indirectly from the use of this product.

This product is provided "As Is" and no warranties are express or implied for this product. Use of this product constitutes acceptance of this "No Liability" policy and the Terms and Conditions as stipulated in this document, which cover each and every part of the product, provided in this package including but not limited to the core product, bonuses and affiliate materials. If you do not agree with this policy, you are not permitted to use this product and must immediately delete this product from your computer or storage device.

Applicable law may not allow the exclusion or limitation of liability or incidental or consequential damages. As such, the above limitation or exclusion may not apply to you. The liability for damages, regardless of the form of action, shall not exceed the fee paid for the product.

WARRANTIES:

There are **No Warranties** express or implied and **Specifically no Warranties** regarding the fitness for specific purpose or **Warranty of Merchant Ability** of this product.

MATERIAL CONNECTION/AFFILIATE DISCLAIMER:

You should assume that the author and publisher have an affiliate relationship and/or another material connection to the providers of goods and services mentioned in this guide and may be compensated when you purchase from a provider. You should always perform due diligence before buying goods or services from anyone via the Internet or offline.

Ron Kness.com may receive compensation from some of the entities listed in this report for referrals, as their "thank you" for sending you their way. However, Ron Kness.com never recommends any service or product solely for the reason of receiving commissions (and neither should you) – We know our reputation is on the line!